THE SUBCONSCIOUS ADJUSTMENT

UNLOCKING THE LAW OF ATTRACTION AND UNDERSTANDING THE POWER OF YOUR THOUGHTS

LINDA LAWLER

1

ISBN-13:978-1496045232
ISBN-10:14960452

DEDICATION

This book is dedicated to my husband Noah. His love raised my vibrational level to want to actively pursue my passion of positively impacting people. I thought a book would be the best way to reach more people. With his support I've been able to finish writing this book I've started a while ago. We have learned a lot from each other over the years. I've learned that the bond between a loving and committed husband and wife can overcome any obstacle or challenge. He has been one of my greatest manifestations by far. We have an unstoppable force known as a MASTERMIND.

Thank you for keeping my love tank full. I love you Noah!

"One day, in your search for happiness, you discover a partner by your side, and you realize that your happiness has come to help you search. To find someone who will love you for no reason, and to shower that person with reasons, that is the ultimate happiness."

Robert Brault

DISCLAIMER

The information provided in this book is designed to provide helpful information on the subjects discussed. This book is designed to provide information and motivation to the reader. This book is not meant to be used, nor should it be used, to diagnose or treat any medical condition. No warranties or guarantees are expressed or implied by the author. The author is not liable for any physical, psychological, emotional, financial, incidental, consequential or other damages. You are responsible for your own choices, actions, and results.

CONTENTS

ACKNOWLEDGEMENTS

I would like to first of all thank my dad, Kevin Lawler. He started teaching me about the Law of Attraction when I was a little girl. He passed away before I was able to fully understand the concepts.

I would like to express my gratitude for my mom being my number one supporter and cheerleader. She has made me feel like anything is possible.

I am very thankful that Marion Lopez put the book "The Secret" in my hand. She helped me to remember the teachings my dad started and helped guide me through the challenges and opportunities in my life.

I want to especially thank the Global Information Network for all of the teachings and trainings I've received about the truth and introducing me to B.E.S.T.

I want to thank Morter Health System for certifying me as a B.E.S.T. Practitioner and allowing me to be part of their mission to 'improve the health of mankind worldwide'. I want to specifically thank Dr. M.T. Morter Jr., Dr. Ted Morter, Dr. Tom Morter, Dr. Sue Morter, Dr. Roland Philips, Cheryl Philips, Melissa Higby (Mel) and Sunny who gave me my first B.E.S.T. adjustment.

I would like to thank all the organizations I've been a part of and all the people I've met on this path. Every encounter and situation has made me who I am today and taught me valuable lessons on this journey we call life. You know who you are.

FOREWORD

Is your life the way you want it to be? Have you tried to make changes with no results? The Subconscious Adjustment by Linda Lawler is a must read. I like to consider myself very knowledgeable about the Law of Attraction and I still learned something new. Linda's knowledge of the Law of Attraction and B.E.S.T. is quite impressive and she shares much of this knowledge in this well written book. She explains everything in an easy to understand and interesting way. She uses lots of examples that clarify the steps involved.

Linda Lawler is a certified B.E.S.T. practitioner that has helped many people overcome pain, anxiety, and self-sabotage tendencies. She clearly explains the benefits of a B.E.S.T. treatment to achieve your health, wealth and relationship goals. B.E.S.T. is also the adjustment people need in order to activate the Law of Attraction. Many people fail to manifest their desires because it isn't synced to the subconscious mind. I highly endorse B.E.S.T. and believe you should get an adjustment as often as you can.

Now although I have only known Linda for a few years it is obvious that she has a definite purpose in life to positively impact people. What better way to positively impact people than by providing optimal health and helping people achieve their dreams and desires. She has such a burning desire to help people and loves it so much that it doesn't feel like work to her.

Linda has manifested and overcome many challenges in her life all thanks to her positive mind set. She feels very strongly about you taking charge of your life. What if you had the best health you've ever had? What if you could have, be and do anything you desired? With this book, Linda hopes to help you shift your mind set and show you how to intentionally create the life and health you've always wanted.

The Subconscious Adjustment: Unlocking the Law of Attraction and Understanding the Power of Your Thoughts is a treasure chest of tools and knowledge to take 100% control of your life and live a happy life of intent and purpose. As a success coach I wish I knew about the benefits of B.E.S.T years ago and plan to recommend it to all my clients.

This book will give you better health.
Gauranteed
This book will give you a happy life.
Gauranteed
This book will give you all that you desire.
Gauranteed

If you don't experience a positive and dramatic difference in your life you may need to read this book again or even a few more times. Now, this powerful book is in your hands. Dive into it, especially if there are things in your life that you want to change. As a final benefit, Linda has gathered together for you some special bonuses and powerful tools. You can access them effortlessly by simply following the simple directions in the book.

Raymond Aaron
New York Times Best Selling Author

PREFACE FROM THE AUTHOR

My education on the Law of Attraction started when I was a little girl. I was privileged to have a dad that new the truths and the secrets of the Universe. My training ended when my dad passed away from Congested Heart Failure (CHF) when I was 17. His teachings that I still remember are:

1. You are and will become what you think about most of the time
2. Be a giver. The more you give the more you get
3. Don't let money stop you from doing what you want in life
4. The truth is whatever you say is the truth
5. Walk in like you own the place
6. The problem isn't the problem, it's how you handle the problem that is the problem
7. You can have anything you want just not when you want it
8. I won' tell you to do anything you can't do.
9. You have a shell around you that people can see
10. Go on a cruise every year. You need to treat yourself
11. Good things happen to good people and bad things happen to bad people
12. Great people talk about ideas, average people talk about things, and mediocre people talk about other people
13. Don't use crutches when you don't need it or soon you'll need it
14. You create your own reality
15. Never answer a question with "I don't know", it is better to say "I don't know but I will find out"

Since then I've been on a journey to learn the truth and master the law of attraction. I've had many challenges and opportunities over the years. Getting a B.E.S.T. treatment was a pivotal point in my life. Getting a subconscious adjustment and getting rid of blockages made it easier to manifest with the Law of Attraction and gave me optimal health and a happy life.

One opportunity in particular was getting certified as a B.E.S.T. practitioner. I am now able to significantly change the lives of people in a positive way. It would have been nice to have known about B.E.S.T when my dad was experiencing heart issues. I believe he would still be alive today. Everyone that ever knew him would only have positive things to say about him. It is so rewarding to be able to change people's lives and save lives with B.E.S.T. If you know anyone that is miserable and suffers from pain or an illness, you should suggest them look into B.E.S.T.

"Always pass on what you have learned"
Yoda

I'm not writing this book saying I know everything. I am sharing what I have learned, my experiences, and what has worked for me to live a happy life with intent. This book is for those that want change for the better in any area and aspect of their life. Turn the page with an open mind and a willingness to learn.

INTRODUCTION

"You must unlearn what you have learned"
Yoda

Before you read this book I want you to think about your willingness to learn and accept change. Reading this introduction says a little bit to your willingness to learn. Many people skip everything before chapter 1 when they read a book. Finishing this book will determine your willingness to learn, while putting what you've learned into practice demonstrates your willingness to accept change. The topics and concepts in this book may go against a lot of your core beliefs, understanding and programming. In order for you to get the most out of this book you need to proceed with an unbiased view point.

I am going to introduce to Bio energetic synchronization technique (B.E.S.T.) which is an energetic balancing that removes interference from the subconscious. I will then explain the difference between your conscious and subconscious mind. Next I will cover how everything is energy and then the importance of thoughts and emotions. I will explain the science behind the Law of Attraction as well as activating the Law of Creation. I will show you how to recognize success and how to increase you vibrations. With understanding and implementation of these teachings you will be on your way to being a manifesting master.

You need to take 100% responsibility of your life. Everything that happens to you is a product of your thoughts. You attracted the positive and negative people and situations in your life. You have the power to change your life.

To learn more about balancing your mind/body, unlocking the law of attraction and understanding the power of your thoughts, check out my website at www.subconsciousadjustment.com.

"Your thoughts have the power to change your health and life. When you see someone's circumstances, you see inside their mind. Therefore, to change your health or life, you must adjust your subconscious.*"*

Linda Lawler

Chapter 1

WHAT IS B.E.S.T?

"At this time we should actively, without conscious thought, speed up brain activity to heighten all physiological processes for survival"
Dr. M.T. Morter Jr.

B.E.S.T is a physical yet non-forceful, energy balancing procedure used by the hands to reestablish the full healing potential of the body using its natural healing abilities. This technique and technology was developed over 30 years ago by Dr. M.T. Morter Jr., with the mission to *"improve the health of mankind worldwide"*. He has adjusted the royal families, presidents to Dr. Wayne Dyer, Jack Canfield, Dr. Michael Beckwith any countless more with energetic healing. His life will be remembered as one that changed the way to a healthy mind and body. I feel privileged to have trained directly from him.

The best definition of B.E.S.T is that it removes the interference and distractions that are demanding the attention of the healing power; thereby causing the imbalance in the autonomic nervous system, and ultimately leading to disease. This healing method is also beneficial and effective on animals.

Researched at major universities, taught in association with many chiropractic colleges and in professional continuing education seminars, B.E.S.T is recognized by the health care industry as an effective healing science. B.E.S.T. is widely used by health care practitioners all over the world who practice mind/body healing, and who recognize the body is more than the sum of its parts.

Dr. Sue Morter explains it as; the body reveals short-circuited neurological patterns as a result of unresolved subconscious emotional issues, affecting all systems required for health and wholeness. Those patterns can be demonstrated as tight muscles, dysfunctional organs or glands, emotional stress or depression type reactions. By accessing areas of the brain through a pressure point type therapy, that is, touching certain points around the head and body in a specific sequence, while having you think about certain memory stresses, the body begins to reconnect the circuitry with the brain. Clinical experience has shown that by stimulating these specific pressure points as part of the B.E.S.T. procedure, your body can not only begin to feel better, but will actually begin to repair and rebuild.

"The secret of health for both mind and body is not to mourn for the past, not to worry about the future, or not to anticipate troubles, but to live in the present moment wisely and earnestly"
Buddha

Everything the body does is for the sole purpose of survival, right now. It isn't designed to be sick or healthy. It is designed to survive the conditions of the moment, and it deals with these conditions by responding to the greatest threat to survival first, whatever is in top priority.

For example, if you experience a physical or emotional trauma your body goes into flight or fight mode. Once this circumstance is over with, your subconscious mind needs to update the current status. If something isn't done to update the current status of the threat and remove the interference created, your body's response is stuck and keeps responding over and over to old information causing that particular system to become exhausted. Exhaustion of a system is what leads to pain, ailments and disease. By touching certain key pressure points in the proper sequence with proper energy and identifying the associated feeling, interference is removed from the subconscious. This results in body balancing, healing of ailments and disease as well as syncing your subconscious mind with your goals. Your body will be ready to run at its optimal potential.

For example, let's discuss someone with muscle tightness. That muscle tightness was appropriate for a previous situation but is no longer needed at the present time. If muscle is tight for too long it will cause exhaustion of systems and organs that will change the way they function. This is observed when someone faces a physical or emotional trauma which causes the mind/body to be in fight or flight mode.

B.E.S.T. is updating how your past experience is stored in the subconscious mind. This adjustment is not telling the person to forget the memory, but instead neutralizing the interference associated with the negative experience.

Signs you may need a B.E.S.T. treatment are:

-Have a disease/illness

-Suffer from chronic or occasional pain

-Tired/fatigued all of the time

-Difficulty losing weight

-Loss of range in motion of your body

-Feelings of depression, anxiety, bi-polar

-Feeling your life is in a rut

B.E.S.T. is an effective method to:

- activate the Law of Attraction

- pain relief and body adjustments

- expand your energy field

- change the frequency/vibrations you transmit

- sync subconscious with goals/desires

- end self-sabotaging tendencies

- natural balancing of nervous system

- remove blocked negative energy

- help heal and recover from surgery

- optimal health, energy, peace of mind and happiness

-Prenatal and postnatal care for mother and baby

The path toward permanent relief must include finding the root of the pain or distress. Often, the actual cause is not obvious, because pain can be located in one part of the body while the cause may be located in another. This is why the western medicine practice of taking a pill to stop symptoms is doing more harm than good. Symptoms from a headache, high blood pressure and rashes are just a few of the ways your body is trying to tell you something isn't right.

Cause of distress occurs from three areas: trauma, toxicity, and thoughts. This means stress from injury, dietary insufficiencies, or emotional reactions that cause interference in your body. In all cases, the actual cause of pain or distress must be identified and corrected so symptoms do not return. With a B.E.S.T. treatment you will be able to identify the feeling behind the distress and neutralize it.

There is active and passive healing. The western world of medicine is run as passive healing. Take this pill to make the symptoms go away, is a total disregard to the cause of the symptoms and what your body is trying to tell you. B.E.S.T. is an active healing process. You must do something in order to get better. The things you need to work on are:

1. What you think
2. What you eat
3. What you drink
4. What and how you breathe
5. How you exercise
6. How you rest

Through daily changes in the choices you make, you can dramatically change your health and life.

Other components to active healing are forgiveness, abdominal breathing, and the Morter March. Forgiveness is very important. In order to move forward in life you need to let go of all negative emotions in your past and present. Understand that all stress is an unlearned lesson, while disappointment is just things that are not in our control that don't go as expected. Abdominal breathing helps change the pattern from survival mode to health mode. The Morter March is an exercise that helps improve neurological balance and can be discussed further during your B.E.S.T session.

Case Study #1

A woman was experiencing severe pain in her knee. It would swell up for a few days, then go back down, and then swell up for a week. After a few weeks of excruciating pain, the woman went to a doctor. The doctor injected cortisone into her knee and it made the pain go away.

A few months later the cortisone wore off and her knee hurt even more than it originally did. The doctor injected more cortisone and it was good for another few months. When her knee swelled up again it tore the meniscus of the knee and she was told she would need surgery. After surgery her knee was locked and was very painful. The doctor reported the surgery wasn't a success and that she would need a knee replacement.

She wanted to get a second opinion and got a B.E.S.T. treatment. She was told that her knee swelling was a direct response to a past negative experience. The feeling associated with the experience was identified, contact points were made and the interference was removed. Upon standing up from the adjustment table her knee was 95% better. Tears of joy rolled down her face as she walked around the room. Her husband was in disbelief and even more shocked at the speed in which her own body repaired her knee.

Case Study #2

A new mom had a 6 month old baby that didn't sleep longer than 30 minutes since she was born. She brought her daughter in for a B.E.S.T. treatment and it was discovered that the baby was operating in flight or fight mode from injuries during the birthing process. The baby received a B.E.S.T. treatment and slept for 18 hours and grew up to be a happy baby.

When we respond negatively to the stress we see it manifest as physical pain or negative circumstances. Identifying stress and its impact will help you respond appropriately to future situations. We are all made up of energy and are connected energetically. Nothing happens to our physical body that did not first happen to the energy body. For example, if a parent is upset, their child can experience sudden neck pain. The child picks up on it energetically.

A B.E.S.T. treatment is not a one-time thing. That's thinking like the people that go to the gym once and feel so good they don't feel the need to go back. Many of us can attest to that. They're not going to get the desired results. Even a chiropractor recommends treatment a few times a month to see consistent results. Once you experience a trauma, toxin or negative thought your mind/body is unbalanced again. It is only when you reach unconscious competence that you can maintain a longer balance of a B.E.S.T. treatment.

Chapter 2

EVERYTHING IS ENERGY

*"Everything is energy and that's all there is to it.
Match the frequency of the reality you want and you
cannot help but get that reality. It can be no other
way. This is not philosophy. This is physics"*
Albert Einstein

The law of energy was revealed to us by
scientists and quantum physicians. According to
Albert Einstein and Thomas Edison, the law states
that everything is energy, vibrating at a different
frequency. Everything that seems to be solid is really
just impulses of energy moving at a certain
frequency. Everything you see and touch is made up
of 99.99% energy.

It has been proven by quantum physics that
energy cannot be created nor destroyed but can
change form. This means that everything we want in
life already exists in some form of energy. One must
learn to harness and direct energy to create their
reality.

Albert Einstein and Thomas Edison have also
concurred that the brain is a transmitter that emits
and receives frequency. These frequencies travel
through steel and mortar which when focused is
picked up by other brains. This happens
instantaneously with frequency bypassing space and
time. It has been scientifically proven by many more
quantum physicists that your brain can transmit with
low power or blast with large amounts of power like
a volume knob similar to that of a radio transmitting
frequency.

The difference is that human frequency is stronger and goes in all directions, not just bouncing off satellite towers. Whatever frequency you emit the same frequency is drawn to you.

Electricity is a form of energy we use every day. This substance is something we cannot see but it is manageable and measured. How does your cell phone work? How does your T.V. work? It works by transmitting and receiving electrical energy just like your brain. You don't need to understand how it works, just know that it does work. If you want to know more about energy you can research much of Einstein's and Tesla's work and be amazed of what they knew.

"If you want to find the secrets of the universe, think in terms of energy, frequency and vibration"
Nikola Tesla

It has been scientifically proven that you have an electromagnetic field around your body. This energy field has been documented and described as pulsating. Similar to a vascular pulse, this pulse is evident throughout development and may be the determining factor in cell differentiation.   During a B.E.S.T. treatment, the pulse is detectable at each contact point. Synchronizing and balancing of this pulse signifies the updating of information stored in the subconscious mind.

Nothing happens to the physical body that doesn't first happen to the energy field. The energy field can be seen through special technology as well as through the human eye, which has become known as an aura. You need to expand your energy field to feel more energetic and attract the health and life you want. Quantum physics has explained why energetic healing is being used so widely and is extremely effective.

"Your thoughts create your soul energy field and affect everything about your very existence"
Dr. M.T. Morter Jr.

Chapter 3

CONSCIOUSLY PROGRAM YOUR SUBCONSCIOUS

"The body is the servant of the mind. It obeys the operations of the mind, whether they be deliberately chosen or automatically expressed"
James Allen

Your mind is divided in two parts, conscious and subconscious. If comparing it to an iceberg, the subconscious mind is like the part of the iceberg you cannot see but is the largest and most powerful part. There is the conscious mind that is aware of the current situation. You think, make decisions and rationalize and analyze consciously. It is estimated that your conscious mind runs 5% of your life, while the subconscious mind runs the other 95%.

The subconscious mind stores information. It operates through pictures and feelings. You can recall this information once you think about it. You can picture it as a vault full of memories, good and bad. Once you repeat something enough, it becomes engrained in your subconscious. This can be seen when you can recite your phone number and address or when you drive home and don't remember most of the drive. Accessing the subconscious mind is like being on auto pilot. No thought is required.

Another way your subconscious is activated is if an emotion, thought, word, smell or situation triggers a past memory. Some experience this as déjà vu. Your beliefs are turned into your reality by the subconscious mind.

"Your beliefs become your thoughts,
Your thoughts become your words,
Your words become your actions,
Your actions become your habits,
Your habits become your values,
Your values become your destiny."

Ghandi

So if you want to change your actions you have to think about it enough to make it a habit. It takes about 45 days to truly create a habit. This is why New Year's resolutions usually fail. Someone will get a few days or weeks in and give up. There were not enough results produced to motivate you to continue. If they just persisted consistently for a few more weeks they would have made a dramatic lifestyle change.

Unfortunately we live in a microwave generation where people want instant results. But as the age old saying goes, "everything worthwhile takes time and patience".

"No problem can be solved from the same level of consciousness that created it"
Albert Einstein

There are four stages to learning:

1. Unconscious incompetence which means you don't know what you don't know. For example, someone that doesn't know about the law of attraction and the power of their thoughts.

2. Conscious incompetence is when you know you don't know. For example, someone who has learned about the law of attraction but doesn't know how to make it work with intention.

3. Conscious competence is achieved when you are in the process of learning. For example, someone who has learned the techniques of activating the law of attraction and is putting it into practice.

4. Unconscious competence is the final stage where you can do something without even thinking about it. This is the stage where you are functioning with your subconscious. For example, someone who has become a master of their thoughts and emotions can manifest their desires like its second nature.

"Don't allow your mind to tell your heart what to do. The mind gives up easily"
Paulo Coelho

B.E.S.T reprograms the subconscious for optimal mind/body function and syncing desires with the subconscious mind. When your subconscious is not on the same page with the conscious your mind is transmitting a frequency of intention as well as counter intention.

Some examples can be seen when you are trying to lose weight but you overeat and aren't very active or if you want to get out of debt but you continue to charge your credit cards with unnecessary purchases. These situations are labeled as being distracted, self-sabotaging or lazy. In order to get your actions in line with your desires you need to get your subconscious on board. If you have hit a plateau or become stagnant in life, B.E.S.T. can give you a gentle reboot.

"Insanity: Doing the same thing over and over again and expecting different results"
Albert Einstein

Chapter 4

THINK ABOUT YOUR THOUGHTS

"You become what you think about most of the time"
Earl Nightingale

The Law of Transmutation explains that energy moves in and out of physical form. Thoughts are creative energy and are actual particles. The more you focus your thinking on what you desire, the more you harness your creative power to move that energy into results in your life. The Universe organizes itself according to your thoughts. Put your energy, effort, thoughts and actions into attracting what you desire, and you will surely attract the physical manifestation of that energy.

"Since you alone are responsible for your thoughts, only you can change them"
Paramhansa Yogananda

Your thoughts play a major role in your health. Think about something or someone that really bothers you. Your body will experience an increase in its heart rate. The shoulders will tense up, headaches or even feelings of nausea can occur just by thinking about it. It works the same way when you think about someone you love. Just your thoughts can make you smile and you get that warm fuzzy feeling inside.

"Every unpleasant thought is a bad thing literally put in the body"
Prentice Mulford

Can you see how what you think can actually change your bodily function? Each emotion causes a chemical release. Negativity for example causes the body to produce cortisol. Cortisol is known to suppress the immune system, increases blood pressure, shuts down reproductive system, reduces bone formation, stimulates gastric acid secretion; impair learning, and fat accumulation around the waist. When you think negative thoughts for too long you have an excess of chemicals at a dangerous level.

All chemicals have an appropriate time and place. If you are running from danger you go into flight or fight mode. Adrenaline is released that makes you go faster meanwhile slowing digestion which is both perfect responses to the situation. Adrenaline is not a good thing when you are trying to sleep. Do you ever sleep through the night, yet wake up even more tired? This means that your subconscious is running programs that don't need to be active.

In today's world our major stressors aren't running from lions, tigers and bears. Our new stressors are; I'm going to be late for work, I don't want to get fired, is my significant other cheating on me. If you are stressed about paying bills it's not a one-time thought. You are stressing and worrying about your bill for days, weeks, months or even years.   A B.E.S.T. treatment can bring you back to zero and have your body only producing chemicals that are needed for the current environment.

"I admit thoughts influence the body"
Albert Einstein

Thoughts are so powerful it is said that one can think themselves thin or 'think and grow rich'. When your thinking is right you can attract like-minded thoughts and actions. There must be congruency with thoughts and actions. These thoughts can change your DNA, health, and reality. Everything starts with a thought. Thoughts can be seen as an actual particle. Your thoughts are a reflection of your life. Negative people have negative circumstances while positive people have positive circumstances. Thoughts alter our emotions.

"Whatever the mind of man can believe and bring itself to believe it can achieve"
Napoleon Hill

Our thoughts shape our perception that creates our reality. Misperception can be dangerous. An example of this is when an anorexic person looks in the mirror. They see an overweight person while the rest of the world sees someone who is skin and bones. The perception of an anorexic person triggers their brain to send a chemical to the body to reduce weight. Misperception can be a matter of life or death. Our perception changes not only our reality but also our biology and genes. It has been scientifically proven that your mind can change your physiology and cause/cure disease. This can be done through a B.E.S.T. adjustment.

There is a widely accepted fact that a pregnant woman's thoughts and emotions are so powerful and important that they affect the baby in the wound and has an impact on development.

Another proven concept of the power of thought is the placebo effect. Studies have been done that show that a test group that was given a sugar pill had more of a significant improvement than those that took the medication. The reasoning behind this is the medication is used to mask symptoms while also causing additional side effects.

We've all heard those commercials for pharmaceutical drugs where they hurriedly name all the negative side effects from diarrhea to death. Even worse are the commercials you hear that say if you've been taking this medicine stop taking it immediately and call "this number". Medicine has become a scary gamble of Russian roulette. No illness or disease was a result of a lack in medicine.

Now I'm not saying all medicine is bad, there are certain lifesaving drugs and procedures. Majority of Americans are on multiple medications; ranging from anti-depressants, pain relievers, blood pressure medicine, blood thinners, cholesterol medicine, etc. Living off several pills a day for the rest of your life is not living. It is highly recommended that one does not abruptly stop taking prescribed medications. Work with your doctor on your plan to wean off medications while also working with a B.E.S.T. practitioner to get your body to naturally do what it was designed to do.

"A man is but a product of his thoughts, what he thinks he becomes"
Ghandi

What do you say to yourself? What do you say to others? I challenge you to try to be positive for 45 days. If you find yourself thinking negatively, say "cancel, cancel" and think of a more positive thought about the situation. It's not going to be easy but there are positive things you can find in any situation. For example, if someone asks you how was dinner. Would you say the food was terrific, or would you focus on the long wait and high prices?

Many will argue that they are just being realistic when it comes to their negativity. But one can counter with "When you focus on the positive you attract more positive people and situations into your life. When you focus your thoughts on the negative, you attract more negative people and situations into your life." This is known as like attracts like and it is a universal law known as the law of attraction. I will go in to this law further in this book.

"Talking about our problems is our greatest addiction. Break the habit, talk about your joys"
Rita Schiano

Chapter 5

MONITORING YOUR EMOTIONS

"That which you give energy and your emotion to becomes your reality. Whatever you give your emotion to becomes reality for you"
Kiesha Crowther

Your emotional IQ is determined by your ability to control and express your emotions. Do you react or respond to a situation? In order to start being in control of your emotions you must learn to respond instead of reacting. This takes time and lots of practice. You can think of it as working towards a Zen like or Yoda demeanor. There should be no situation or person that should get a rise out of you. If you do you are giving that person power and only hurting yourself.

"Anger is the most impotent of passions. It effects nothing it goes about, and hurts the one who is possessed by it more than the one against whom it is directed"
Carl Sandburg

This is a well-known quote that holds truth. A thought triggers an emotion. It is up to you what emotion you feel. Below is a list of negative emotions and chemicals that are released.

Anger = Norepinephrine
Panic = Dopamine
Hostility = 35 multiple chemicals
Negativity = Cortisol

Having too much of the above chemicals in your body acts as a poison and effects how your mind and

33

body function. On the other hand positive emotions release chemicals such as oxytocin, serotonin and endorphins.

"Feelings do not grow old along with the body. Feelings form part of a world I don't know, but it's a world where there's no time, so space, no frontiers"
Paulo Coelho

A great way to monitor your emotions is to know where you are on the emotional guidance system. Jerry and Esther Hicks have come up with this emotional guidance system and you can learn more about it from their book "Ask and it is Given"

1. Love/Appreciation/Empowered/Freedom
2. Passion
3. Enthusiasm/Eagerness/Happiness
4. Positive Expectation/Belief
5. Optimism
6. Hopefulness
7. Contentment
8. Boredom
9. Pessimism
10. Frustration/Irritation/Impatience
11. Feeling Overwhelmed
12. Disappointment
13. Doubt
14. Worry
15. Blame
16. Discouragement
17. Anger
18. Revenge
19. Hatred/Rage
20. Jealousy
21. Insecurity/Guilt/Unworthiness
22. Fear/Grief/Depression/Despair/Powerlessness

First identify where you are on the emotional guidance system. Your emotions can change throughout the day. What emotions do you predominantly feel? If you are depressed it's going to be a challenge to jump to the feeling of joy. It is easiest to move up the scale at your own pace. Moving from depressed to worry is taking a step in the right direction. Everyday your goal should be to feel as good as you can now and keep feeling better.

In order for your health to be optimal and to have a life you love you have to stay in the upper range of the emotional guidance system. We are all human and our emotions will change throughout the day going up and down the scale. Only by consciously trying to raise your emotional IQ and seeing the positive in everything will you be at conscious competence with your emotions. Until then you will be on an emotional rollercoaster through life.

"Remember, a Jedi's strength flows from the Force. But beware. Anger, fear, aggression. The dark side are they. Once you start down the dark path, forever will it dominate your destiny"

Yoda

Don't get me wrong some people love the ride. These are the people that like to stir things up a bit, some call it drama. There is nothing wrong with that person enjoying that. Everyone is entitlement to live a happy life they enjoy. What gives someone joy may not do the same for another. What someone hates may not bother other people.

Judgment has very negative repercussions. Everyone should just accept people for who they are and if they aren't on the same page with you they will distance themselves from you. But also remember, what you resist persists.

"A day wasted on others is not wasted on one's self"
Charles Dickens

Approach everything and everyone with love and respect. This will drastically change the collective consciousness of us all as a whole and we will be able to fully appreciate the new age of enlightenment.   If you are a certain way, people that are close to your vibrational frequency will be attracted to you. This is why you see cliques, gangs, organizations of like-minded people with common goals. All we humans genuinely want is to be happy, accepted, and to have the freedom to do what they love. To me that is the definition of Success.

Chapter 6

SCIENCE BEHIND THE LAW OF ATTRACTION

"The greatest discovery of our generation is that human beings can alter their lives by altering their attitudes of mind. As you think, so shall you be"
William James

There are several laws of the universe. Quantum physics has proven that the law of lift supersedes the law of gravity, while the law of attraction supersedes all other laws. The law of attraction demonstrates how we attract people and situations into our life. You can have, be, or do anything you think about if you believe. Our thoughts, feelings, words and actions create energy which attracts like energy. Positivity attracts positive people and circumstances while negativity attracts negative people and circumstances. Just like the other universal laws, you don't need to believe in order for the law of attraction to work.

The law of attraction has been used by albert Einstein, Thomas Edison, Thomas Jefferson, Andrew Carnegie, Napoleon Hill, Henry Ford, Jack Canfield, Dr. Wayne Dyer, Dr. Michael Beckwith, Dr. Bruce Lipton, Dr. M.T. Morter Jr, Arnold Schwarzenegger, Will Smith, Jim Carey and countless others that have taken control of their life.

Scientists have proven that our brain transmits frequency 24 hours a day. All you have to do is increase the power, frequency and duration and a matching frequency will come rushing towards you like a magnet. Our magnetic energy field around our body is always attracting people and situations that give you that matching frequency. These frequencies are based off feelings of emotion. Remember, your subconscious operates through pictures and feelings. You want to feel as good as you can to attract positive people and situations.

Many people today are living under the victim mentality. This is the person that is waiting for a chance to sue someone for a large settlement or feels no control and life has just been a sequence of negative circumstances. We all need to take 100% responsibility for our lives. Whether you lose your job, get in a car accident, or get sick, you caused it and it is only you that can remedy it.

This statement will rub many people the wrong way; it is just too far of a jump from your current beliefs and programming. I suggest reading further and try to get a better understanding of something that you aren't too sure about.

"I don't like that man very much; I need to get to know him better"
Abraham Lincoln

You need to be able to recognize your manifestations, intentional or not. Here are some examples of the law of attraction working in your life:

1. You think about an old friend and out of the blue they call you. And you say "I was just thinking about you!"

2. When a women is focusing on the fact that she can't get pregnant and then when she stops trying that is when she becomes pregnant.

3. When a husband is focusing on all the things he doesn't like about his wife and she continues to do things that irritate him vs. the husband that understands that nobody is perfect and focuses on what he loves about his wife and he gets more love from his wife.

4. When you tell your child not to do something and they do more of that which you don't like. Instead of saying don't touch that, avert their attention to something else and say let's play with this.

5. You are frustrated at work and on your way home you get pulled over. Getting pulled over made you feel frustrated, which matched how you felt at work.

6. A friend of yours dies and you worry about one day dying, and you end up in a car accident. You were in fear for your life upon impact. That accident matched the feeling you were putting out of 'fear of death'.

7. You think about how you don't like your job and that you want a new one that pays more. Then you get fired. You put out the frequency that you don't want your job and now that is so. You saw this as a great opportunity and are focusing on the job of your dreams. You apply to several jobs but none of them contact you because they aren't a match to the frequency of the type of job you want. You continue to keep a positive attitude and out of nowhere you get a call about the perfect job for you.

This last scenario doesn't usually play out like this because majority of the people will have such a large ball of negative energy after losing the job. Worrying about bills, feeding your family and the future is not a one-time thing, it pours into your mind all day every day. The focus has to be shifted on the outcome you want with no doubt or impatience.

Now, imagine the amazing life you would have if you went about your day always excited and thankful. You would have a constant flow of people and situations that get you excited and make you feel thankful. This should be your main goal when working the law of attraction. If you're not at the right vibration you can't attract physical things like your dream car, dream job, soul mate, etc.

"Happiness is when what you think, what you say, and what you do are in harmony"
Ghandi

You need be happy first. Happiness is the key to being healthy, manifesting your desires and ultimate success. Most people have it backwards. For example, I'll be happy when I find my soul mate. No, you need to be happy to find your soul mate. You need to do more at work to be considered for a promotion, not get a promotion and then you'll put in more effort.   Once you reach a place of true unaltered happiness you can easily and effortlessly attract your desires.

There is one caveat; you have to believe. When I say believe, I mean you have to believe as if you already have it. This is a hard concept for someone to grasp, especially when one has been without for so long. Think about how you feel when you order a meal at a restaurant. You don't wonder if you'll get what you asked for, there is no doubt or worry. You don't get your order right away, you have to wait.   If you didn't get what you wanted or it wasn't what you expected just simply put in another order.

Majority of the time your expectations have been met from constant and repetitive events in your life. Do you say to yourself "Everything bad always seems to happen to me" or do you exclaim "im so lucky and everything works out in my best interest"? Your feelings are a major component. You need to feel good when you think about your desire.

"Everything is possible for him who believes"
Mark 9:23

"Therefore I tell you, whatever you ask for in prayer, believe that you have received it, and it will be yours"
Mark 11:24

"Ask, and it shall be given you; seek; and you shall find; knock and it shall be opened unto you. For every one that asketh receiveth; and he that seeketh findeth; and to him that knocketh it shall be opened"
Matthew 7:7-8

The law of attraction is congruent with many religions. The law of attraction has been compared to karma. What you sow, you reap. What you put out you get back. Treat others the way you want to be treated.

Chapter 7

ACTIVATE THE LAW OF CREATION

"As you start to walk out on the way, the way appears"
Jalal Rumi

The law of creation is activated once we have a strong desire and high belief. In order to consciously create, one must have faith. Faith is defined as persistence despite no empirical evidence. You create what you focus on. Clearly define your desire and focus on it and know through faith that you will manifest it.

The 5 steps to create:

1. Define what you want
2. Feel good now
3. Realize your true WHY
4. Increase your belief
5. Take immediate action

1. Define what you want

"There is one quality that one must possess to win and that is definite of purpose. The knowledge of what one wants, and a burning desire to possess it"
Napoleon Hill

What is it that you want? Sometimes it is easier to determine what we want when we learn what we don't want. So be thankful for people and situations that teach you the lesson to know what you don't like. Once you know what you don't want, you must turn your back to it and only think about it in a positive way. Being in a state of wanting keeps you in a state of wanting, you need to get to the point of feeling as if you already have it and you are just waiting for the best time for it to come in.

For example, you don't like feeling so tired all the time. You don't want to focus on not being tired, because your focus is on being tired and you will attract more people and circumstances that make you feel tired. Instead your focus should be to have more energy.

Getting your thoughts and desires on paper is an excellent way to expand your dreams. Write out a list of everything you desire and don't factor in money. Be sure to state it in a positive way. Other examples of desires are:

1. A harmonious home life
2. Soul mate
3. Peace of mind
4. Optimal Health
5. High paying job
6. Lose weight

You want to go through your list and choose one desire that you believe you can achieve that you will focus on. We will call this your chief aim. Your chief aim can be very specific, general, or a feeling. Examples of each are:

Specific chief aim- I want to lose 30 lbs

General chief aim- I want to be thinner

Feeling chief aim- I want to feel attractive or I want my clothes to fit better

If you are new to the creation process it is best to focus on feeling with no time limit. This will allow the universe to give you what is best for you with no worry or doubt. It is better to be specific about things that are in abundance and general about things that are limited. But ultimately what is best is what gives you a good feeling and believe in.

Delving further into the above example; if you've tried losing 30 pounds for years, you most likely have negative subconscious programs running. You may notice you gained even more weight when you were trying to lose weight. In this case, it may be a good idea to have a general or feeling chief aim about weight loss. If your mind/body is still running on flight or fight mode from a past physical or emotional trauma, it is going to be a challenge to lose weight.

If your body isn't functioning properly your systems and organs aren't working efficiently or effectively. A B.E.S.T. treatment can be a great tool to reach your ideal weight.

1.   Feel good now

"If you're doing things in order to be happy…you are doing them in the wrong order"
Michael Neill

You need to feel good when you think about your desire. You need to feel as good as you can right now. No matter the situations and circumstances you need to stay positive. Your thoughts can change the outcome of any scenario. Everything you want stems from a desired feeling.

You can skip right to feeling that feeling before you get what you want. Feel as if you would feel when you get what it is you wanted. How would you feel when you get that job, relationship, better health? When you think about why you want something, it can help you feel good. That makes you halfway here. Now all that's left is to get your desire.

If your negative ball of energy is too large to do this step there are things you can do. Such as writing a list of all the things you are thankful and grateful for. Like you have someone in your life that loves you, your bills are getting paid, you have a roof over your head, you can walk, etc. You should also think about your desires along with congruent positive affirmations. The easiest and most effective way is a B.E.S.T. treatment. This will remove the negative blocks of interference in your subconscious mind.

2. Realize your true WHY

"You can have anything you want if you want it badly enough. You can be anything you want to be, do anything you set out to accomplish, if you hold that desire with singleness of purpose"
Abraham Lincoln

Once you have your definite chief aim selected you need to ask yourself why. This is an important step because you need to have a strong enough why to keep you focused on your desire to its fulfillment. Going back to the earlier example, ask yourself, why do I want to lose weight? The reasons could be:

1. To feel better
2. To look better

2. To have more energy
3. To be able to play with my child
4. To be able to run with my dog
5. To fit into my clothes
6.   To be healthier

When your WHY is clear, the HOW will appear.

3. Increase your belief

"Whether you think you can or you think you can't either way you are right"
Henry Ford

Now you need to believe and have no doubt. A popular method of getting ones belief level up is dream building. This is done by getting as close to your desires as possible. Such as test driving your dream car or hanging out with a friend with an active and healthy lifestyle. An additional method to use is a dream book and dream board. These tools help keep you focused on things that give you the same feeling as the feelings your desires will give you.

A dream book is a book you use to write down your desires, affirmations, quotes that resonate with you and also to put pictures of your desires or pictures of things that give you the same feeling as your desires.

For example you and your partner both desire to have a baby. You put pictures of baby stuff or pictures of people with a happy baby. This is specifically how my husband and I manifested our baby.

It is subconsciously more powerful to put yourself in the pictures you look at. You can do this with photo shop or take pictures of you with your desires. You want to look at your dream book as often as possible and update it frequently. It is said that the best times to look at a dream book and board is when you wake up, middle of the day and before you go to bed.

A dream board is similar to a dream book but it should only comprise of pictures. As mentioned earlier, your subconscious mind runs off pictures and feelings. A simple poster board with pictures that match your feelings is a great way to focus.

Your dream board can be beneficial or detrimental. You shouldn't look at it as a board with the all the things you don't have. You will attract more situations that make you feel lack and will always be in a state of wanting. Instead you should look at it and feel good and excited about all the awesome circumstances coming your way.

If you don't feel this way, there is a block in your subconscious. You don't want to look at your dream board until you get a BEST adjustment and get your subconscious synced to your desires.

Now you need to write out your desire as if you already have it and include feeling and emotion of why you want it. You should be focusing on this statement so many times a day that you commit it to memory. Similar to when you have a song stuck in your head that replays over and over.

You may have a few different affirmations you use but they should all be congruent to your chief aim. The key is to focus on one desire at a time.

Here are some examples of chief aims and affirmations:

1.   My chief aim is to be thin

I love feeling so slender and attractive
I love feeling so energetic and getting so much done
I lose weight easily and effortlessly
I am thankful and grateful I am healthy inside and out

2.   My chief aim is to earn $5000 a month

I love being able to help those in need
I'm thankful and grateful I don't owe anyone any money
I'm thankful and grateful for my new car
I attract money easily and effortlessly

It is really beneficial to write your chief aim on one side of an index card and your desire statements on the other side. You should keep this card with you and look at it as often as possible. Reading it out loud with genuine enthusiasm and belief adds to the power and intensity of your vibrational frequency.

Another way to help you stay focused is putting your desire statements on the fridge and your bathroom mirror. Once you feel good and have a high belief of your desire, you are in the sweet spot. A strong and solid WHY increases intensity of emotion and belief which motivates one to act.

3. Take Immediate Action

"The great aim of education is not knowledge but action"
Herbert Spencer

Once you feel good and have a high belief of your desire, you are in the sweet spot. You have your chief aim and are ready to take action to fuel your desire and belief.

Take action as a leap of faith. Actions should make you feel good and increase belief. If the actions don't feel good you need to go back to step 2. An extreme example is someone who quits their job because they are making room in their life for the awesome job coming their way. Other examples are taking a class to learn more about a certain subject your desire is related to or cleaning out your garage to make room for the new car on its way.

Here are examples of actions steps that are congruent with desires:

Health goal: I am thankful and grateful that I feel so slender

Action step #1- Eat more organic food
Action step #2- Workout at least 3 times a week
Action step #3- Cook most of my own meals

Wealth goal: I am thankful and grateful that all my credit cards are paid off

Action step #1- Cut up all my credit cards
Action step #2- Sell or unsubscribe to things I don't need
Action step #3- Get a part time job to bring in another stream on income

Relationship goal: I am thankful and grateful for my happy marriage

Action step #1- Focus on the positive
Action step #2- Communicate and express feelings
Action step #3- Make spouse feel special with surprises

NOTES

NOTES

NOTES

Chapter 8

RECOGNIZE SUCCESS

"Don't aim for success if you want it; just do what you love and believe in, and it will come naturally"
David Frost

You've put in the request for your desire to the universe. Now what? It goes back to feeling good. The Law of Gestation explains that everything takes time to manifest. All things have a beginning and grow into form as more energy is added to it. Thoughts are like seeds planted in our fertile minds that bloom into our physical experience if we have nourished them. You need to stay focused and know that your goals will become reality when the time is right.

Remember the example about ordering food at a restaurant. You know you'll get it when the order is ready, or in your case you'll get it once you are ready. How do you know when you are ready? When you have no doubt or worry about it coming in. Worry is negative goal setting, thinking about what you don't want to happen.

Some people feel good thinking about their desire all day every day. Some people have such high faith and belief that their desire is coming they don't need to think about it all the time. They are feeling as if they already got it. When you get something you've wanted you aren't thinking about getting it. Each person's method depends on how they feel and where they are on the emotional guidance system.

How and where your desire happens or comes from is totally off your radar screen. The way you think it's going to happen usually isn't the way it materializes. The universe is moving mountains to put people and situations in your life that matches the feeling you broadcast. You may have attracted your desire and not recognize it.

You might say *"I didn't attract this house fire",* but what were you feeling about your house?

"I didn't like my house and I wanted a new and bigger one".

The unfortunate house fire is going to result in the insurance money getting you a new house of your choosing. Careful with this one, I experienced this house fire scenario twice growing up with positive outcomes.

The way in which you manifest the matching feeling is off your radar screen and you have no idea how it will happen. Remember the example about wanting a better job and then you lose your current one. We all know the saying be careful what you wish for.

If you are feeling good then the way the situation manifested is the best way it could have happened for you. All day every day you just need to monitor your feelings, because whether you ask or not you are attracting people and situations that give you the matching feeling. It helps to care, but not that much.

For example, if you meet someone that you think is perfect for you, they may not be the best vibrational match for you. There will be situations and circumstances that may appear like a bad or negative thing, but know that thing had to happen to get you what you are broadcasting with your frequency.

For example, you might think you have manifested the perfect job for you, but then it doesn't fall through. There is no need to get upset or frustrated. Either you were transmitting the frequency of worry of not getting the job or there is a better job on its way to you that you cannot even imagine because it is off your radar screen. Despite what you experience you need to stay positive and be thankful. When you feel you have nothing to be thankful for is when you need to be the most thankful.

"When you truly see the good in an unpleasant experience then you will have simultaneously learned the lesson"
Dr. M.T. Morter Jr.

I would like to share a compelling story about a man in China. There was a war going on in China. This man became worried about his son being drafted and becoming a casualty of war. A week later the man's son fell off a horse and broke his leg. Everyone in the town was talking about how horrible the situation was and sending the family their condolences. The man said *"I don't know why, but my son breaking his leg was a good thing"*. A few days later the Chinese Army was rounding up young men to fight in the war. They couldn't take the man's son because of the broken leg,

Another example of a good broadcast is *"I really like Jessica, she might be the one, she may not, but the perfect person for me will come into my life at the perfect time"*. Jessica might be in fact your soul mate or she may have been someone you met to help you clearly define what you want in a partner. This outlook will attract someone who makes you very happy and fills all your needs. Another good broadcast to send out is "I really like this house and I want to buy it, but there might be a better house for me out there". Don't put a limit on your manifestations.

There is a success cycle to manifesting. The more you intentionally manifest what you want your belief level goes up. Success builds confidence. Life is a game and you create the rules. Make it so the rules are easy for you to win.   Keep track of your manifestations and accomplishments. Monitor the increase of things that are measurable like, your bank account growing or the number on the scale going down.

"In order to succeed, your desire for success should be greater than your fear of failure"
Bill Cosby

NOTES

NOTES

NOTES

Chapter 9

RAISING YOUR VIBRATION

"Hard work is not the path to Well- Being. Feeling good is the path to Well-Being. You don't create through action; you create through vibration. And then, your vibration calls action from you"

Abraham Hicks

The Law of Vibration states that everything is vibrating and nothing rests. Vibrations of the same frequency resonate with each other, so like attracts like energy. Everything is energy, including your thoughts. Consistently focusing on a particular thought or idea attracts its vibrational match. You apply this by focusing on what you want instead of what you don't want.

The speed in which you can activate the law of attraction and manifest your desire depends on the power and intensity of the vibrational frequency you are transmitting as well as the duration. If you are also transmitting a block of counter intention such as doubt and fear it will add resistance or even stop the manifestation process.

A B.E.S.T treatment can help increase your vibrations, sync your desire with your subconscious mind and remove all the blocks. Taking drops of Trace Mineral Energy will hold the B.E.S.T. adjustment in place for a longer length of time. You can find these under the products tab at www.Morter.com. Trace Minerals can even replace your morning coffee or energy drink. You will start the day vibrant, alert and energized.

You feed your body every day. Do you feed your mind every day? It is very beneficial to read and listen to something motivating, inspiring and educational each and every day. Here is a list of great books to improve your mind set:

- ➢ The Magic of Thinking Big
- ➢ As a Man Thinketh
- ➢ See You At the Top
- ➢ The Power of Now
- ➢ Ask and It Is Given
- ➢ The Secret
- ➢ The New Psycho-Cybernetics
- ➢ The Law of Success in 16 Lessons
- ➢ Think and Grow Rich
- ➢ The Magic of Believing
- ➢ The Go-Getter
- ➢ The Soul Purpose
- ➢ The Power of Positive Thinking
- ➢ The Game of Work
- ➢ Rich Dad Poor Dad
- ➢ Acres of Diamonds
- ➢ Natural Cures They don't Want You to Know About

Additional ways to raise your vibration:

- Eat organic Do things that make you happy and feel good
- Cleanses: liver, gallbladder, kidney, spleen, colon, parasite, fat cell, candida
- Exercise, stretch, yoga, martial arts, Qi Gong
- Rebounder- Connie David, certified reboundologist can be contacted at codaventerprises@comcast.net
- Vibration plate
- Organize car, home, and work
- Create a dream book/board

- Learn something new
- Associating with positive like-minded people
- Get debt free
- Positively impact as many people as you can
- Saying please and thank you
- Listening to classical music
- Write out goals and affirmations on white paper and blue ink. Different colors vibrate at different frequency
- Keep your body alkaline versus acidic

There are everyday things that are detrimental to your health, lower your vibration and inhibit your ability to manifest. It isn't required that you stop all of these things immediately for it to work. It would be very beneficial, but small everyday changes in your choices will be an easier and better transition. Watch out for:

- Prescription and non-prescription drugs
- Artificial sweeteners like aspartame, splenda, high fructose corn syrup, and monosodium glutamate (MSG)
- Genetically modified food (GMO)
- Corn and corn fed meat and dairy
- Soy beans
- Canola
- Sodas
- Mineral oil
- Vaccines
- Shellfish
- Farm raised fish
- Pork
- Propylene glycol
- Magnesium stearate
- Talc powder

- Chlorine
- Nitrates
- Fluoride
- Sodium laureth sulfate
- Stearic acid
- Hypnosis
- Root canals
- Florescent lights
- Mercury and even mercury fillings

Chapter 10

MANIFESTING MASTER

"Imagination is a force that can actually manifest reality"
James Cameron

After practicing these techniques you can determine if your desires are your own, or if they are desires you were programmed to want through marketing and media. There is more to the law of creation than just attracting stuff. Through my journey of exploring the law of attraction I learned that optimal health, sufficient finances, and great relationships are most important. Life is not really about material gain. Do what you love and live a happy life, no matter the circumstances.

If you don't have what you want, there are only two reasons and they are:

1. You are not focusing on what you want, which is transmitting the wrong frequency.

2. You are transmitting the right frequency but you are also sending out a block. This block can be due to worry, doubt, fear, and signals your subconscious is sending out that you are not aware of.

A B.E.S.T treatment can help you with these two major reasons people are not living the life they want.

Success is a journey not a destination. Success has been programmed in us to mean how much money you have in the bank. People will give away their soul doing something they do not believe in or balancing costs with the well-being of humanity. If you are doing what you love and are happy you have obtained success.

The teacher who teaches because it was her dream and she loves shaping the minds of the future, is a success.

The stay at home mom, who is blissfully happy and loves taking care of her family, is a success.

The auto mechanic who genuinely loves working the inner logistics of a vehicle and is excited about each new vehicle that is back up and working properly, is a success.

The person, who has a passion for singing and has the ability to move people with their voice, is a success.

It is said that the money you are worth is in direct proportion with the number of people you serve. So if you want to earn more money, you must serve more people.

It's not all about the money or the stuff you get; it's about being blissfully happy, having great health, wealth and relationships. Imagine how beautiful the world would be if everyone strived to positively impact as many people as they could. It all starts with your family, then your friends, then community, then country, then the world and finally the universe. Did you make someone feel special today?

"As human beings, our job in life is to help people realize how rare and valuable each one of us really is, that each of us has something that no one else has--or ever will have--something inside that is unique to all time. It's our job to encourage each other to discover that uniqueness and to provide ways of developing its expression."
Mister Rogers

I covered different ways of thinking along with a lot of controversial topics. You may need to read this book a few times to truly understand the message. The main points I hope you walk away with today are:

1. You need a B.E.S.T. treatment
2. Your thoughts effect your health and life's circumstances
3. Associate with positive like-minded people
4. You have an electromagnetic field around you that attracts matching frequency
5. You have control over what you vibrate and you can raise your vibration
6. You are 100% responsible for your current health and life and you are the only one that changes it.
7. Using the law of attraction you can intentionally create the life of your desires
8. You need to master your emotions and feel as good as you can right now
9. To get more positive people and circumstances you need to think more positive
10. Everyday think about what you are thankful and grateful for
11. You can have anything you want, just not exactly when you want it
12. The truth is whatever you say is the truth

13. Choose a desire that gets you excited and you believe in as your ONE main focus.
14. You don't know how your desire is going to come about because it is off your radar screen
15. Recognize when you attract people and circumstance of your desired frequency.

Where is your willingness to learn now? What is your willingness to accept change now?

If you have any questions, go to my website www.subconsciousadjustment.com and submit your question in the contact tab. I look forward to hearing from you and wish you a happy and healthy life.

Made in United States
Troutdale, OR
03/23/2025

29996332R00040